OH MY GOD,
WHAT A COMPLETE DIARY 2021

Gill Books
Hume Avenue
Park West
Dublin 12
www.gillbooks.ie

Gill Books is an imprint of M.H. Gill & Co.
© Emer McLysaght and Sarah Breen 2020
978 07171 9018 8

Designed by grahamthew.com
Printed and bound in Turkey
This book is typeset in Futura Book

This book is a work of fiction. Any references to historical events, real people or real places are used fictitiously. Other names, characters, places and incidents are products of the author's imagination, and any resemblance to actual incidents or persons, living or dead, is entirely coincidental.

The paper used in this book comes from the wood pulp of managed forests.
For every tree felled, at least one tree is planted, thereby renewing natural resources.

All rights reserved.
No part of this publication may be copied, reproduced or transmitted
in any form or by any means, without written permission of the publishers.
A CIP catalogue record for this book is available from the British Library.

5 4 3 2 1

THIS DIARY BELONGS TO

Also by the Authors

OH MY GOD, WHAT A COMPLETE AISLING

THE IMPORTANCE OF BEING AISLING

ONCE, TWICE, THREE TIMES AN AISLING

OH MY GOD,

What a COMPLETE DIARY 2021

—

EMER MCLYSAGHT & SARAH BREEN

—

GILL BOOKS

INTRODUCTION

Hello, and welcome to your new diary. Doesn't it smell nice?

With this little book, we wanted to create a tool to help you stay on top of things. Because if there's one word to describe Aisling, 'organised' would be it. But we didn't want it to be just a place to jot down birthdays, we wanted it to be a friend, a little companion to help you plan and prioritise the things that are important to you.

Aisling has always kept a diary. In school, it was where she detailed her rows and laughs with Majella and mused over which member of Westlife she fancied the most. Later, it became a safe place to offload the day's stresses and confess that she only ever really had eyes for Shane. Journaling, as the Yanks call it, has been proven to reduce stress and have lots of other benefits too.

After kicking off with an Aisling-tastic inspirational quote, every month is laid out over two pages so you can tell at a glance how many baby showers you have or when your car tax is due. There's also a space for you to write the month's attainable, measurable goals that you can then prioritise. Do you want to take up Zumba? Or learn 'Maniac 2000' on the tin whistle? Get out your Good Pen and write it down. It's all about being intentional. And then, once you achieve your goals, you get to tick them off, which is really the only reason to make a list in the first place.

Every week is laid out over two pages, and there's space for your Important Bits. Here's where you can keep track of your daily life and socialising. Once you get into the habit of using it, we're hoping you won't be able to imagine your life without it, sort of like how ludicrous the world would be without smartphones or Dolmio Stir In.

We've all been through a fierce time this past year, and we understand more than ever the importance of a little bit of structure every day. We want you to strive when it's time for you to strive, rest when it's time for you to rest, and smell the roses when it's time to smell the roses (usually in May and June. Put it in the diary right now).

Good Luck!

Emer and Sarah

2021 AT A GLANCE

JANUARY

M	T	W	T	F	S	S
				1	2	3
4	5	6	7	8	9	10
11	12	13	14	15	16	17
18	19	20	21	22	23	24
25	26	27	28	29	30	31

FEBRUARY

M	T	W	T	F	S	S
1	2	3	4	5	6	7
8	9	10	11	12	13	14
15	16	17	18	19	20	21
22	23	24	25	26	27	28

MARCH

M	T	W	T	F	S	S
1	2	3	4	5	6	7
8	9	10	11	12	13	14
15	16	**17**	18	19	20	21
22	23	24	25	26	27	28
29	30	31				

APRIL

M	T	W	T	F	S	S
			1	2	3	4
5	6	7	8	9	10	11
12	13	14	15	16	17	18
19	20	21	22	23	24	25
26	27	28	29	30		

MAY

M	T	W	T	F	S	S
					1	2
3	4	5	6	7	8	9
10	11	12	13	14	15	16
17	18	19	20	21	22	23
24	25	26	27	28	29	30
31						

JUNE

M	T	W	T	F	S	S
	1	2	3	4	5	6
7	8	9	10	11	12	13
14	15	16	17	18	19	20
21	22	23	24	25	26	27
28	29	30				

PUBLIC HOLIDAYS 2021

1 January 2021, Friday, New Year's Day
17 March 2021, Wednesday, St Patrick's Day
5 April 2021, Monday, Easter Monday

3 May 2021, Monday, May Bank Holiday
7 June 2021, Monday, June Bank Holiday

2021 AT A GLANCE

JULY

M	T	W	T	F	S	S
			1	2	3	4
5	6	7	8	9	10	11
12	13	14	15	16	17	18
19	20	21	22	23	24	25
26	27	28	29	30	31	

AUGUST

M	T	W	T	F	S	S
						1
2	3	4	5	6	7	8
9	10	11	12	13	14	15
16	17	18	19	20	21	22
23	24	25	26	27	28	29
30	31					

SEPTEMBER

M	T	W	T	F	S	S
		1	2	3	4	5
6	7	8	9	10	11	12
13	14	15	16	17	18	19
20	21	22	23	24	25	26
27	28	29	30			

OCTOBER

M	T	W	T	F	S	S
				1	2	3
4	5	6	7	8	9	10
11	12	13	14	15	16	17
18	19	20	21	22	23	24
25	26	27	28	29	30	31

NOVEMBER

M	T	W	T	F	S	S
1	2	3	4	5	6	7
8	9	10	11	12	13	14
15	16	17	18	19	20	21
22	23	24	25	26	27	28
29	30					

DECEMBER

M	T	W	T	F	S	S
		1	2	3	4	5
6	7	8	9	10	11	12
13	14	15	16	17	18	19
20	21	22	23	24	**25**	**26**
27	28	29	30	31		

2 August 2021, Monday, August Bank Holiday
25 October 2021, Monday, October Bank Holiday
25 December 2021, Saturday, Christmas Day
26 December 2021, Sunday, St Stephen's Day

2021 GOALS

2021 GOALS

HOLIDAY PLANNER

Is there anything better than planning all your holidays for the year – and booking the days off before anyone else? Hello endorphins!

HOLIDAY PLANNER

Happy New Year! The best way to beat the January blues is by spending all your Christmas vouchers (even if they don't expire for five years. Thank you, Consumer Protection [Gift Vouchers] Act 2019)

January

JANUARY AT A GLANCE

28 MONDAY	29 TUESDAY	30 WEDNESDAY	31 THURSDAY
1 FRIDAY	**2** SATURDAY	**3** SUNDAY	**4** MONDAY
5 TUESDAY	**6** WEDNESDAY	**7** THURSDAY	**8** FRIDAY
9 SATURDAY	**10** SUNDAY	**11** MONDAY	**12** TUESDAY
13 WEDNESDAY	**14** THURSDAY	**15** FRIDAY	**16** SATURDAY

JANUARY AT A GLANCE

17 SUNDAY	18 MONDAY	19 TUESDAY	20 WEDNESDAY
21 THURSDAY	22 FRIDAY	23 SATURDAY	24 SUNDAY
25 MONDAY	26 TUESDAY	27 WEDNESDAY	28 THURSDAY
29 FRIDAY	30 SATURDAY	31 SUNDAY	1 MONDAY
2 TUESDAY	3 WEDNESDAY	4 THURSDAY	5 FRIDAY

ALL ABOUT JANUARY

*D*espite the atrocious weather, I've always had a soft spot for January. Something about having the slate wiped clean appeals to my inner primary teacher. New beginnings. A fresh start. Time to get the head down.

But, of course, you can't be too hard on yourself, not when it's dark for 18 hours a day and the rain is coming at you sideways. You'd crack up. Majella is already in my ear about doing Dry January and upping our daily steps to 15,000 but, honestly, life is too short, I told her. I'd rather be kind to myself and ease into 2021 gently. And if that involves a cheeky little Pinot Greej on a Friday, then so be it. Maybe I'll even be able to twist her arm.

ALL ABOUT JANUARY

GOALS FOR JANUARY

NEW THINGS TO READ/ WATCH/MAKE/EAT

MUST GET DONE

SELF-CARE IDEAS

JANUARY 1–3

28 MONDAY **DECEMBER**

29 TUESDAY

30 WEDNESDAY

31 THURSDAY

1 FRIDAY **JANUARY** NEW YEAR'S DAY

Time to practise writing 2021 without making a hames of it. If last night was a late one, take two paracetamol and remember tomorrow is another day.

JANUARY

2 SATURDAY

3 SUNDAY

IMPORTANT BITS

M	T	W	T	F	S	S
				1	2	3
4	5	6	7	8	9	10
11	12	13	14	15	16	17
18	19	20	21	22	23	24
25	26	27	28	29	30	31

JANUARY 4–10

4 MONDAY

5 TUESDAY

6 WEDNESDAY NOLLAIG NA MBAN

Traditionally when us gals get to relax after all of last month's festivities. I'll be bringing Mammy out for a cup of tea and a cream cake.

7 THURSDAY

8 FRIDAY

JANUARY

9 SATURDAY

10 SUNDAY

IMPORTANT BITS

M	T	W	T	F	S	S
				1	2	3
4	5	6	7	8	9	10
11	12	13	14	15	16	17
18	19	20	21	22	23	24
25	26	27	28	29	30	31

JANUARY 11–17

11 MONDAY

12 TUESDAY

13 WEDNESDAY

14 THURSDAY

15 FRIDAY

JANUARY

16 SATURDAY

17 SUNDAY

IMPORTANT BITS

M	T	W	T	F	S	S
				1	2	3
4	5	6	7	8	9	10
11	12	13	14	15	16	17
18	19	20	21	22	23	24
25	26	27	28	29	30	31

JANUARY 18–24

18 MONDAY

19 TUESDAY

20 WEDNESDAY

21 THURSDAY

22 FRIDAY

JANUARY

23 SATURDAY

24 SUNDAY

IMPORTANT BITS

M	T	W	T	F	S	S
				1	2	3
4	5	6	7	8	9	10
11	12	13	14	15	16	17
18	19	20	21	22	23	24
25	26	27	28	29	30	31

JANUARY 25–31

25 MONDAY

26 TUESDAY

27 WEDNESDAY

28 THURSDAY

29 FRIDAY

JANUARY

30 SATURDAY

31 SUNDAY

IMPORTANT BITS

M	T	W	T	F	S	S
				1	2	3
4	5	6	7	8	9	10
11	12	13	14	15	16	17
18	19	20	21	22	23	24
25	26	27	28	29	30	31

JANUARY REFLECTIONS

JANUARY REFLECTIONS

If snowdrops can make it out of the ground in February, then you can make it out of the bed on a frosty morning. Gloves on, windscreen defrosted, cheeks red, let's go!

February

FEBRUARY AT A GLANCE

1 MONDAY	**2** TUESDAY	**3** WEDNESDAY	**4** THURSDAY
5 FRIDAY	**6** SATURDAY	**7** SUNDAY	**8** MONDAY
9 TUESDAY	**10** WEDNESDAY	**11** THURSDAY	**12** FRIDAY
13 SATURDAY	**14** SUNDAY	**15** MONDAY	**16** TUESDAY
17 WEDNESDAY	**18** THURSDAY	**19** FRIDAY	**20** SATURDAY

FEBRUARY AT A GLANCE

21 SUNDAY	22 MONDAY	23 TUESDAY	24 WEDNESDAY
25 THURSDAY	26 FRIDAY	27 SATURDAY	28 SUNDAY
1 MONDAY	2 TUESDAY	3 WEDNESDAY	4 THURSDAY
5 FRIDAY	6 SATURDAY	7 SUNDAY	8 MONDAY
9 TUESDAY	10 WEDNESDAY	11 THURSDAY	12 FRIDAY

ALL ABOUT FEBRUARY

January can feel like an eternity, so I like to greet the first day of February like an old friend. 'Come in,' I say. 'I know you're very wet and cold but aren't you a step in the right direction?' It's a short month too and somehow that makes it seem friendly. That might be cracked, to call a month friendly, but me and February have always been pals. This February isn't a leap year but on the 28th of the month (or the 29th, if we're in luck) me and the girls always indulge in an annual rewatch of the classic film *Leap Year* starring Amy Adams and the hot lad with the ferocious accent who shows up for Lady Mary at the end of *Downtown Abbey*. That's probably a spoiler for *Downtown Abbey* but if you haven't caught up by now there's no hope for you.

February is the month for Valentines too, of course, but I haven't paid much heed since I caught Mammy sending me a card from 'a secret admirer' when I was in third year. My trust in the holiday was shattered forever because those cards had been coming for at least six years and I had attributed them to half the lads in BGB.

ALL ABOUT FEBRUARY

GOALS FOR FEBRUARY

NEW THINGS TO READ/WATCH/MAKE/EAT

MUST GET DONE

SELF-CARE IDEAS

FEBRUARY 1–7

1 MONDAY IMBOLC / ST BRIGID'S DAY

My favourite St Brigid tradition (not forgetting the cross and the Brídeóg, I'm not an animal) is leaving out some fabric for B herself to bless. Great for a sore throat or a vicious hangover.

2 TUESDAY

3 WEDNESDAY

4 THURSDAY

5 FRIDAY

FEBRUARY

6 SATURDAY

7 SUNDAY

IMPORTANT BITS

M	T	W	T	F	S	S
1	2	3	4	5	6	7
8	9	10	11	12	13	14
15	16	17	18	19	20	21
22	23	24	25	26	27	28

FEBRUARY 8–14

8 MONDAY

9 TUESDAY

10 WEDNESDAY

11 THURSDAY

12 FRIDAY GALENTINE'S EVE

Tomorrow is Galentine's Day, and as noted Aisling Leslie Knope says, 'Galentine's Day is about celebrating lady friends. It's wonderful and should be a national holiday.' She's right! I might start a petition!

FEBRUARY

13 SATURDAY GALENTINE'S DAY

14 SUNDAY

IMPORTANT BITS

M	T	W	T	F	S	S
1	2	3	4	5	6	7
8	9	10	11	12	13	14
15	16	17	18	19	20	21
22	23	24	25	26	27	28

FEBRUARY 15–21

15 MONDAY

16 TUESDAY PANCAKE TUESDAY

I'm one of the few people left in the world who honours tradition and only has pancakes once a year on this special day. And get away from me with your savoury fillings. Sacrilege!

17 WEDNESDAY

18 THURSDAY

19 FRIDAY

FEBRUARY

20 SATURDAY

21 SUNDAY

IMPORTANT BITS

M	T	W	T	F	S	S
1	2	3	4	5	6	7
8	9	10	11	12	13	14
15	**16**	**17**	**18**	**19**	**20**	**21**
22	23	24	25	26	27	28

FEBRUARY 22–28

22 MONDAY

23 TUESDAY

24 WEDNESDAY

25 THURSDAY

26 FRIDAY

FEBRUARY

27 SATURDAY

28 SUNDAY

IMPORTANT BITS

M	T	W	T	F	S	S
1	2	3	4	5	6	7
8	9	10	11	12	13	14
15	16	17	18	19	20	21
22	23	24	25	26	27	28

FEBRUARY REFLECTIONS

FEBRUARY REFLECTIONS

Spring is here and with it the chance to bloom. The clocks go forward on the 28th and nothing says 'blooming' like changing the time in the car and on the microwave at your earliest convenience.

March

MARCH AT A GLANCE

1 MONDAY	**2** TUESDAY	**3** WEDNESDAY	**4** THURSDAY
5 FRIDAY	**6** SATURDAY	**7** SUNDAY	**8** MONDAY
9 TUESDAY	**10** WEDNESDAY	**11** THURSDAY	**12** FRIDAY
13 SATURDAY	**14** SUNDAY	**15** MONDAY	**16** TUESDAY
17 WEDNESDAY	**18** THURSDAY	**19** FRIDAY	**20** SATURDAY

MARCH AT A GLANCE

21 SUNDAY	22 MONDAY	23 TUESDAY	24 WEDNESDAY
25 THURSDAY	26 FRIDAY	27 SATURDAY	28 SUNDAY
29 MONDAY	30 TUESDAY	31 WEDNESDAY	1 THURSDAY
2 FRIDAY	3 SATURDAY	4 SUNDAY	5 MONDAY
6 TUESDAY	7 WEDNESDAY	8 THURSDAY	9 FRIDAY

ALL ABOUT MARCH

The first month of spring was always a busy one on the farm what with all the new life kicking off. Most of my childhood memories involve wiggly lambs warming under the red light, feeding sucky calves from a bottle and poor Daddy struggling to stay awake during *Home and Away*. He was never able for the late nights.

I'll be up to ninety myself this year getting the BallyGoBrunch float ready for BGB's St Patrick's Day parade. If I can rope Mad Tom into dusting off his leprechaun costume, there's a good chance we'll get onto the *Six One* regional parades round-up. Although hopefully this year it will be for all the right reasons. Say a prayer for me.

ALL ABOUT MARCH

GOALS FOR MARCH

NEW THINGS TO READ/WATCH/MAKE/EAT

MUST GET DONE

SELF-CARE IDEAS

MARCH 1–7

1 MONDAY

2 TUESDAY

3 WEDNESDAY

4 THURSDAY

5 FRIDAY

MARCH

6 SATURDAY

7 SUNDAY

IMPORTANT BITS

M	T	W	T	F	S	S
1	2	3	4	5	6	7
8	9	10	11	12	13	14
15	16	17	18	19	20	21
22	23	24	25	26	27	28
29	30	31				

MARCH 8–14

8 MONDAY INTERNATIONAL WOMEN'S DAY

Majella tried to use this as an excuse to drink wine last year but I just sent her Malala's Wikipedia page and a picture of Mary Robinson.

9 TUESDAY REMINDER!

It's Mother's Day this Sunday, so if you're celebrating, be sure to hit the shops early or you'll be stuck with a 'Mom' or a 'Mum' card. No self-respecting mammy wants to wake up to that.

10 WEDNESDAY

11 THURSDAY

12 FRIDAY

MARCH

13 SATURDAY

14 SUNDAY MOTHER'S DAY

IMPORTANT BITS

M	T	W	T	F	S	S
1	2	3	4	5	6	7
8	9	10	11	12	13	14
15	16	17	18	19	20	21
22	23	24	25	26	27	28
29	30	31				

MARCH 15–21

15 MONDAY

16 TUESDAY

17 WEDNESDAY ST PATRICK'S DAY

Don't forget to show your patriotism with a hunk of shamrock the size of a dinner plate on your lapel.

18 THURSDAY

19 FRIDAY

MARCH

20 SATURDAY

21 SUNDAY

IMPORTANT BITS

M	T	W	T	F	S	S
1	2	3	4	5	6	7
8	9	10	11	12	13	14
15	16	17	18	19	20	21
22	23	24	25	26	27	28
29	30	31				

MARCH 22–28

22 MONDAY

23 TUESDAY

24 WEDNESDAY

25 THURSDAY

26 FRIDAY

MARCH

27 SATURDAY

28 SUNDAY

IMPORTANT BITS

M	T	W	T	F	S	S
1	2	3	4	5	6	7
8	9	10	11	12	13	14
15	16	17	18	19	20	21
22	23	24	25	26	27	28
29	30	31				

MARCH 29–31

29 MONDAY

30 TUESDAY

31 WEDNESDAY

1 THURSDAY **APRIL**

2 FRIDAY

MARCH

3 SATURDAY

4 SUNDAY

IMPORTANT BITS

M	T	W	T	F	S	S
1	2	3	4	5	6	7
8	9	10	11	12	13	14
15	16	17	18	19	20	21
22	23	24	25	26	27	28
29	30	31				

MARCH REFLECTIONS

MARCH REFLECTIONS

Sweet April showers bring forth May flowers. So just remember every time you're absolutely lashed on during April, it's just another chance to grow (and change into those spare socks you brought in your handbag).

April

APRIL AT A GLANCE

29 MONDAY	30 TUESDAY	31 WEDNESDAY	1 THURSDAY
2 FRIDAY	3 SATURDAY	4 SUNDAY	5 MONDAY
6 TUESDAY	7 WEDNESDAY	8 THURSDAY	9 FRIDAY
10 SATURDAY	11 SUNDAY	12 MONDAY	13 TUESDAY
14 WEDNESDAY	15 THURSDAY	16 FRIDAY	17 SATURDAY

APRIL AT A GLANCE

18 SUNDAY	**19** MONDAY	**20** TUESDAY	**21** WEDNESDAY
22 THURSDAY	**23** FRIDAY	**24** SATURDAY	**25** SUNDAY
26 MONDAY	**27** TUESDAY	**28** WEDNESDAY	**29** THURSDAY
30 FRIDAY	1 SATURDAY	2 SUNDAY	3 MONDAY
4 TUESDAY	5 WEDNESDAY	6 THURSDAY	7 FRIDAY

ALL ABOUT APRIL

Get ready to hear a lot of people saying 'how is it April already?' because it's the first month that really sneaks up on you. 'Sure it's nearly June and then the year is half over,' is another one likely to be rolled out. No point in wishing your life away, though, and if there's anything I learned from that meditation app Majella made me download to deal with my road rage (how hard is it to indicate on a roundabout, though, I ask you?) it's that April is a wonderful month to do a bit of mindful walking. I know, I know, mindfulness seems like a bit of a cod dreamed up by Gwyneth Paltrow but with the trees starting to bloom and everything really popping out in time for summer, I love to take a stroll and pay attention to the nature around me. Just don't forget the umbrella! Oh, and if you don't fire 'April 25th is my perfect date. Because it's not too hot, not too cold and all you need is a light jacket' up on Facebook are you even alive?

ALL ABOUT APRIL

GOALS FOR APRIL

NEW THINGS TO READ/ WATCH/MAKE/EAT

MUST GET DONE

SELF-CARE IDEAS

APRIL 1–4

29 MONDAY MARCH

30 TUESDAY

31 WEDNESDAY

1 THURSDAY APRIL APRIL FOOL'S DAY

Look, I'm no fan of pranks but I have been known to sneak a plastic spider into the Special K. A classic.

2 FRIDAY GOOD FRIDAY

Always reminds me of the time we had a live Stations of the Cross on BGB's main street. Jesus fell for the second time at the bus stop and then met the women of Jerusalem at Filan's shop.

APRIL

3 SATURDAY

4 SUNDAY EASTER SUNDAY

IMPORTANT BITS

M	T	W	T	F	S	S
			1	2	3	4
5	6	7	8	9	10	11
12	13	14	15	16	17	18
19	20	21	22	23	24	25
26	27	28	29	30		

APRIL 5–11

5 MONDAY EASTER BANK HOLIDAY

6 TUESDAY

7 WEDNESDAY

8 THURSDAY

9 FRIDAY

APRIL

10 SATURDAY

11 SUNDAY

IMPORTANT BITS

M	T	W	T	F	S	S
			1	2	3	4
5	6	7	8	9	10	11
12	13	14	15	16	17	18
19	20	21	22	23	24	25
26	27	28	29	30		

APRIL 12–18

12 MONDAY

13 TUESDAY

14 WEDNESDAY

15 THURSDAY

16 FRIDAY

APRIL

17 SATURDAY

18 SUNDAY

IMPORTANT BITS

M	T	W	T	F	S	S
			1	2	3	4
5	6	7	8	9	10	11
12	13	14	15	16	17	18
19	20	21	22	23	24	25
26	27	28	29	30		

APRIL 19–25

19 MONDAY

20 TUESDAY

21 WEDNESDAY

22 THURSDAY

23 FRIDAY

APRIL

24 SATURDAY

25 SUNDAY

IMPORTANT BITS

M	T	W	T	F	S	S
			1	2	3	4
5	6	7	8	9	10	11
12	13	14	15	16	17	18
19	20	21	22	23	24	25
26	27	28	29	30		

APRIL 26–30

26 MONDAY

27 TUESDAY

28 WEDNESDAY

29 THURSDAY

30 FRIDAY

APRIL

1 SATURDAY **MAY**

2 SUNDAY

IMPORTANT BITS

M	T	W	T	F	S	S
			1	2	3	4
5	6	7	8	9	10	11
12	13	14	15	16	17	18
19	20	21	22	23	24	25
26	27	28	29	30		

APRIL REFLECTIONS

APRIL REFLECTIONS

'Ne'er cast a clout till May is out' are words I live by. It's better to be sweating in a coat you can take off than shivering with nothing to put on you.

May

MAY AT A GLANCE

26 MONDAY	27 TUESDAY	28 WEDNESDAY	29 THURSDAY
30 FRIDAY	**1** SATURDAY	**2** SUNDAY	**3** MONDAY
4 TUESDAY	**5** WEDNESDAY	**6** THURSDAY	**7** FRIDAY
8 SATURDAY	**9** SUNDAY	**10** MONDAY	**11** TUESDAY
12 WEDNESDAY	**13** THURSDAY	**14** FRIDAY	**15** SATURDAY

MAY AT A GLANCE

16 SUNDAY	**17** MONDAY	**18** TUESDAY	**19** WEDNESDAY
20 THURSDAY	**21** FRIDAY	**22** SATURDAY	**23** SUNDAY
24 MONDAY	**25** TUESDAY	**26** WEDNESDAY	**27** THURSDAY
28 FRIDAY	**29** SATURDAY	**30** SUNDAY	**31** MONDAY
1 TUESDAY	2 WEDNESDAY	3 THURSDAY	4 FRIDAY

ALL ABOUT MAY

May is my annual reminder that change is in the air. And I'm not talking about the smell of silage (although there's no mistaking it on a warm evening) — it's been a historic month these past few years. We had the marriage equality referendum in 2015 and then the landslide vote to repeal the eighth amendment in 2018. I still get very emotional on the anniversaries, soft touch that I am. Both mighty days for the parish and the country.

I always begin Bealtaine by leaving a little bunch of flowers on the doorstep like Mammy taught me. Nobody wants evil in the house. Then, at the end of the month, and not a minute beforehand, I'll be packing up my black tights and good work shumpers and taking out all my summer bits. Linen trousers? Check. Tankini? Check. The half-price sandals I got in the Clarks sale? CHECK. And that reminds me, the time to get my hooves seen to is now!

ALL ABOUT MAY

GOALS FOR MAY

NEW THINGS TO READ/ WATCH/MAKE/EAT

MUST GET DONE

SELF-CARE IDEAS

MAY 1-2

26 MONDAY **APRIL**

27 TUESDAY

28 WEDNESDAY

29 THURSDAY

30 FRIDAY

MAY

1 SATURDAY **MAY**

2 SUNDAY

IMPORTANT BITS

M	T	W	T	F	S	S
					1	2
3	4	5	6	7	8	9
10	11	12	13	14	15	16
17	18	19	20	21	22	23
24	25	26	27	28	29	30
31						

MAY 3–9

3 MONDAY MAY BANK HOLIDAY

It's not a summer bank holiday if you don't end up eating a 99 after a trek around a local hill. Raspberry syrup on mine, please.

4 TUESDAY INTERGALACTIC STAR WARS DAY

May the fourth be with you. Gas altogether.

5 WEDNESDAY

6 THURSDAY

7 FRIDAY

MAY

8 SATURDAY

9 SUNDAY

IMPORTANT BITS

M	T	W	T	F	S	S
					1	2
3	4	5	6	7	8	9
10	11	12	13	14	15	16
17	18	19	20	21	22	23
24	25	26	27	28	29	30
31						

MAY 10-16

10 MONDAY

11 TUESDAY

12 WEDNESDAY

13 THURSDAY

14 FRIDAY

MAY

15 SATURDAY

16 SUNDAY

IMPORTANT BITS

M	T	W	T	F	S	S
					1	2
3	4	5	6	7	8	9
10	**11**	**12**	**13**	**14**	**15**	**16**
17	18	19	20	21	22	23
24	25	26	27	28	29	30
31						

MAY 17–23

17 MONDAY

18 TUESDAY

19 WEDNESDAY

20 THURSDAY

21 FRIDAY

MAY

22 SATURDAY

23 SUNDAY

IMPORTANT BITS

M	T	W	T	F	S	S
					1	2
3	4	5	6	7	8	9
10	11	12	13	14	15	16
17	18	19	20	21	22	23
24	25	26	27	28	29	30
31						

MAY 24–30

24 MONDAY INTERNATIONAL BROTHER'S DAY

I tend to use this day to remind my brother about International Sister's Day, which is the first Sunday in August. Paul, if you're reading this, I enjoy a scented candle. And stop reading my diary!

25 TUESDAY

26 WEDNESDAY

27 THURSDAY

28 FRIDAY

MAY

29 SATURDAY

30 SUNDAY

IMPORTANT BITS

M	T	W	T	F	S	S
					1	2
3	4	5	6	7	8	9
10	11	12	13	14	15	16
17	18	19	20	21	22	23
24	25	26	27	28	29	30
31						

MAY 31

31 MONDAY

1 TUESDAY **JUNE**

2 WEDNESDAY

3 THURSDAY

4 FRIDAY

MAY

5 SATURDAY

6 SUNDAY

IMPORTANT BITS

M	T	W	T	F	S	S
					1	2
3	4	5	6	7	8	9
10	11	12	13	14	15	16
17	18	19	20	21	22	23
24	25	26	27	28	29	30
31						

MAY REFLECTIONS

MAY REFLECTIONS

With the longest day and the shortest night, June shows us that anything is possible. Even the first leg shave of the season without taking the ankles off yourself. #Believe

June

JUNE AT A GLANCE

31 MONDAY	1 TUESDAY	2 WEDNESDAY	3 THURSDAY
4 FRIDAY	5 SATURDAY	6 SUNDAY	7 MONDAY
8 TUESDAY	9 WEDNESDAY	10 THURSDAY	11 FRIDAY
12 SATURDAY	13 SUNDAY	14 MONDAY	15 TUESDAY
16 WEDNESDAY	17 THURSDAY	18 FRIDAY	19 SATURDAY

JUNE AT A GLANCE

20 SUNDAY	21 MONDAY	22 TUESDAY	23 WEDNESDAY
24 THURSDAY	25 FRIDAY	26 SATURDAY	27 SUNDAY
28 MONDAY	29 TUESDAY	30 WEDNESDAY	1 THURSDAY
2 FRIDAY	3 SATURDAY	4 SUNDAY	5 MONDAY
6 TUESDAY	7 WEDNESDAY	8 THURSDAY	9 FRIDAY

ALL ABOUT JUNE

June days are some of the most beautiful days of the year. That's why they have the Leaving Cert in June, out of pure spite. We're guaranteed at least a week of good weather and I can look forward to Majella's bumper crop of 'Best Teacher Ever' presents. She's delighted that it's mostly graduated from mugs and statues to wine and chocolate, but there's always at least one who gets her an embroidered hand towel which she cries over while drinking all the wine.

Every year I promise myself I'll book myself in to Newgrange for one of the solstices but I'm always too late. Maybe now is the time to get on the list for December? I must Google it.

June is traditionally Cemetery Sunday month too, so we'll be off to Daddy's grave with the slug pellets and geraniums so we don't make a show of him. Mrs Dunphy is in the grave next door and it's done up like Graceland but instead of Elvis they're worshipping an eighty-eight-year-old chain smoker. RIP.

ALL ABOUT JUNE

GOALS FOR JUNE

NEW THINGS TO READ/ WATCH/MAKE/EAT

MUST GET DONE

SELF-CARE IDEAS

JUNE 1–6

31 MONDAY MAY

1 TUESDAY JUNE

2 WEDNESDAY

3 THURSDAY

4 FRIDAY

JUNE

5 SATURDAY

6 SUNDAY

IMPORTANT BITS

M	T	W	T	F	S	S
	1	2	3	4	5	6
7	8	9	10	11	12	13
14	15	16	17	18	19	20
21	22	23	24	25	26	27
28	29	30				

JUNE 7–13

7 MONDAY JUNE BANK HOLIDAY

8 TUESDAY

9 WEDNESDAY

10 THURSDAY

11 FRIDAY

JUNE

12 SATURDAY

13 SUNDAY

IMPORTANT BITS

M	T	W	T	F	S	S
	1	2	3	4	5	6
7	8	9	10	11	12	13
14	15	16	17	18	19	20
21	22	23	24	25	26	27
28	29	30				

JUNE 14–20

14 MONDAY

15 TUESDAY NADINE COYLE'S BIRTHDAY

'What dayt of birth did ay say now? Fafteenth of the saxth nineteen eddy faive?'

16 WEDNESDAY

17 THURSDAY REMINDER!

It's Father's Day on Sunday, so if you'll be celebrating, get ready to let him talk about the great picture on the new telly, how sick he is of people leaving lights on, and how good The Shawshank Redemption *is.*

18 FRIDAY

JUNE

19 SATURDAY

20 SUNDAY FATHER'S DAY

IMPORTANT BITS

M	T	W	T	F	S	S
	1	2	3	4	5	6
7	8	9	10	11	12	13
14	15	16	17	18	19	20
21	22	23	24	25	26	27
28	29	30				

JUNE 21–27

21 MONDAY

22 TUESDAY

23 WEDNESDAY

24 THURSDAY

25 FRIDAY

JUNE

26 SATURDAY

27 SUNDAY

IMPORTANT BITS

M	T	W	T	F	S	S
	1	2	3	4	5	6
7	8	9	10	11	12	13
14	15	16	17	18	19	20
21	22	23	24	25	26	27
28	29	30				

JUNE 28–30

28 MONDAY

29 TUESDAY

30 WEDNESDAY

1 THURSDAY **JULY**

2 FRIDAY

JUNE

3 SATURDAY

4 SUNDAY

IMPORTANT BITS

M	T	W	T	F	S	S
	1	2	3	4	5	6
7	8	9	10	11	12	13
14	15	16	17	18	19	20
21	22	23	24	25	26	27
28	29	30				

JUNE REFLECTIONS

JUNE REFLECTIONS

A great poet once wrote
'oh my my my, oh my my my,
oh my my my my, July,' and I
honestly couldn't have put it
better myself.

July

JULY AT A GLANCE

28 MONDAY	29 TUESDAY	30 WEDNESDAY	**1** THURSDAY
2 FRIDAY	**3** SATURDAY	**4** SUNDAY	**5** MONDAY
6 TUESDAY	**7** WEDNESDAY	**8** THURSDAY	**9** FRIDAY
10 SATURDAY	**11** SUNDAY	**12** MONDAY	**13** TUESDAY
14 WEDNESDAY	**15** THURSDAY	**16** FRIDAY	**17** SATURDAY

JULY AT A GLANCE

18 SUNDAY	**19** MONDAY	**20** TUESDAY	**21** WEDNESDAY
22 THURSDAY	**23** FRIDAY	**24** SATURDAY	**25** SUNDAY
26 MONDAY	**27** TUESDAY	**28** WEDNESDAY	**29** THURSDAY
30 FRIDAY	**31** SATURDAY	1 SUNDAY	2 MONDAY
3 TUESDAY	4 WEDNESDAY	5 THURSDAY	6 FRIDAY

ALL ABOUT JULY

Between hens, matches, weddings, festivals, races and the obligation to have rosé with the girls every time the sun comes out, there's hardly a chance to catch your breath in July. But as much as I love being busy, I've learned that being flat-out without a break takes its toll. So I always like to pencil in a little day to myself before the month is out.

The perfect Mé Féin Day involves a lie-in, tea and toast in bed, catching up on my admin, at least three loads of washing, a new nightie, a facemask and an early night with the soaps. Try it and thank me later.

ALL ABOUT JULY

GOALS FOR JULY

NEW THINGS TO READ/ WATCH/MAKE/EAT

MUST GET DONE

SELF-CARE IDEAS

JULY 1–4

28 MONDAY **JUNE**

29 TUESDAY

30 WEDNESDAY

1 THURSDAY **JULY**

2 FRIDAY

JULY

3 SATURDAY

4 SUNDAY

IMPORTANT BITS

M	T	W	T	F	S	S
			1	2	3	4
5	6	7	8	9	10	11
12	13	14	15	16	17	18
19	20	21	22	23	24	25
26	27	28	29	30	31	

JULY 5-11

5 MONDAY

6 TUESDAY

7 WEDNESDAY

8 THURSDAY

9 FRIDAY

JULY

10 SATURDAY

11 SUNDAY

IMPORTANT BITS

M	T	W	T	F	S	S
			1	2	3	4
5	6	7	8	9	10	11
12	13	14	15	16	17	18
19	20	21	22	23	24	25
26	27	28	29	30	31	

JULY 12–18

12 MONDAY

13 TUESDAY

14 WEDNESDAY BASTILLE DAY

Time to brush off your Leaving Cert French. I did German, but can wheel out 'Ou est le gare? Ou est le centre de Georges Pompidou?' when necessary.

15 THURSDAY

16 FRIDAY

JULY

17 SATURDAY

18 SUNDAY

IMPORTANT BITS

M	T	W	T	F	S	S
			1	2	3	4
5	6	7	8	9	10	11
12	13	14	15	16	17	18
19	20	21	22	23	24	25
26	27	28	29	30	31	

JULY 19–25

19 MONDAY

20 TUESDAY

21 WEDNESDAY

22 THURSDAY

23 FRIDAY

JULY

24 SATURDAY

25 SUNDAY

IMPORTANT BITS

M	T	W	T	F	S	S
			1	2	3	4
5	6	7	8	9	10	11
12	13	14	15	16	17	18
19	20	21	22	23	24	25
26	27	28	29	30	31	

JULY 26–31

26 MONDAY GALWAY RACES

Three days of control pants, bubbles and fivers each way in Ballybrit. We missed it last year but put on the fascinators for a socially distant drink in the garden.

27 TUESDAY

28 WEDNESDAY

29 THURSDAY

30 FRIDAY

JULY

31 SATURDAY

1 SUNDAY AUGUST

IMPORTANT BITS

M	T	W	T	F	S	S
			1	2	3	4
5	6	7	8	9	10	11
12	13	14	15	16	17	18
19	20	21	22	23	24	25
26	27	28	29	30	31	

JULY REFLECTIONS

JULY REFLECTIONS

August is sometimes described as the Sunday of summer, but don't let the fear overtake you! Roast a chicken, put some ice-cream in a wafer and make the most of every day.

August

AUGUST AT A GLANCE

26 MONDAY	27 TUESDAY	28 WEDNESDAY	29 THURSDAY
30 FRIDAY	31 SATURDAY	**1** SUNDAY	**2** MONDAY
3 TUESDAY	**4** WEDNESDAY	**5** THURSDAY	**6** FRIDAY
7 SATURDAY	**8** SUNDAY	**9** MONDAY	**10** TUESDAY
11 WEDNESDAY	**12** THURSDAY	**13** FRIDAY	**14** SATURDAY

AUGUST AT A GLANCE

15 SUNDAY	16 MONDAY	17 TUESDAY	18 WEDNESDAY
19 THURSDAY	20 FRIDAY	21 SATURDAY	22 SUNDAY
23 MONDAY	24 TUESDAY	25 WEDNESDAY	26 THURSDAY
27 FRIDAY	28 SATURDAY	29 SUNDAY	30 MONDAY
31 TUESDAY	1 WEDNESDAY	2 THURSDAY	3 FRIDAY

ALL ABOUT AUGUST

August is the spiritual month of the Rose of Tralee, a festival I've been enamoured with since I first saw a Rose remove her long skirt to reveal a shorter skirt underneath to allow her to lep around better while doing her jig. I'm too old to be a Rose now (discrimination at its finest) but if I was to take part my talent would be getting the cover on a kingsize duvet in under 40 seconds (the world record is 39. I'm determined to beat it). It's all in the elbows. August can be peak wedding season. I had four one August. Two were on the same day in neighbouring counties and I managed to make it to both meals. Lovely beef at one. Disappointing chicken at the other. Very dry. One of the other weddings was on a Wednesday. I nearly didn't give a card.

My friend Sadhbh is trying to get me to go to Ibiza this August but I've looked up the weather and there's no way I'd survive that heat. Besides, Sadhbh's idea of a holiday is getting up at 6pm to get ready to go clubbing and I'd want to have visited some sort of castle or monastery and burned the shape of my sandals onto my feet by then. We've agreed to go to Paris for a weekend in October. I didn't do French for my Leaving but I know most of the lyrics to 'Joe le Taxi'.

ALL ABOUT AUGUST

GOALS FOR AUGUST

NEW THINGS TO READ/WATCH/MAKE/EAT

MUST GET DONE

SELF-CARE IDEAS

AUGUST 1

26 MONDAY **JULY**

27 TUESDAY

28 WEDNESDAY

29 THURSDAY

30 FRIDAY

AUGUST

31 SATURDAY

1 SUNDAY **AUGUST**

IMPORTANT BITS

M	T	W	T	F	S	S
						1
2	3	4	5	6	7	8
9	10	11	12	13	14	15
16	17	18	19	20	21	22
23	24	25	26	27	28	29
30	31					

AUGUST 2–8

2 MONDAY AUGUST BANK HOLIDAY

RIP to the summer bank holidays. Make this one count with some cremated sausages on the BBQ, even if it's raining.

3 TUESDAY

4 WEDNESDAY

5 THURSDAY

6 FRIDAY

AUGUST

7 SATURDAY

8 SUNDAY

IMPORTANT BITS

M	T	W	T	F	S	S
						1
2	3	4	5	6	7	8
9	10	11	12	13	14	15
16	17	18	19	20	21	22
23	24	25	26	27	28	29
30	31					

AUGUST 9–15

9 MONDAY

10 TUESDAY

11 WEDNESDAY

12 THURSDAY

13 FRIDAY

AUGUST

14 SATURDAY

15 SUNDAY

IMPORTANT BITS

M	T	W	T	F	S	S
						1
2	3	4	5	6	7	8
9	10	11	12	13	14	15
16	17	18	19	20	21	22
23	24	25	26	27	28	29
30	31					

AUGUST 16–22

16 MONDAY

17 TUESDAY

18 WEDNESDAY

19 THURSDAY

20 FRIDAY

AUGUST

21 SATURDAY

22 SUNDAY

IMPORTANT BITS

M	T	W	T	F	S	S
						1
2	3	4	5	6	7	8
9	10	11	12	13	14	15
16	17	18	19	20	21	22
23	24	25	26	27	28	29
30	31					

AUGUST 23–29

23 MONDAY

24 TUESDAY

25 WEDNESDAY

26 THURSDAY

27 FRIDAY

AUGUST

28 SATURDAY

29 SUNDAY

IMPORTANT BITS

M	T	W	T	F	S	S
						1
2	3	4	5	6	7	8
9	10	11	12	13	14	15
16	17	18	19	20	21	22
23	24	25	26	27	28	29
30	31					

AUGUST 30-31

30 MONDAY

31 TUESDAY ANNIVERSARY OF THE FIRST ROSE OF TRALEE

Won by Dublin Rose Alice O'Sullivan, the 1959 event had no escorts and the budget was just 750 pounds.

1 WEDNESDAY SEPTEMBER

2 THURSDAY

3 FRIDAY

AUGUST

4 SATURDAY

5 SUNDAY

IMPORTANT BITS

M	T	W	T	F	S	S
						1
2	3	4	5	6	7	8
9	10	11	12	13	14	15
16	17	18	19	20	21	22
23	24	25	26	27	28	29
30	31					

AUGUST REFLECTIONS

AUGUST REFLECTIONS

The leaves are changing
and falling and turning to
shite. If trees can let go of
dead weight and still stand tall,
so can you!

September

SEPTEMBER AT A GLANCE

30 MONDAY	31 TUESDAY	1 WEDNESDAY	2 THURSDAY
3 FRIDAY	4 SATURDAY	5 SUNDAY	6 MONDAY
7 TUESDAY	8 WEDNESDAY	9 THURSDAY	10 FRIDAY
11 SATURDAY	12 SUNDAY	13 MONDAY	14 TUESDAY
15 WEDNESDAY	16 THURSDAY	17 FRIDAY	18 SATURDAY

SEPTEMBER AT A GLANCE

19 SUNDAY	**20** MONDAY	**21** TUESDAY	**22** WEDNESDAY
23 THURSDAY	**24** FRIDAY	**25** SATURDAY	**26** SUNDAY
27 MONDAY	**28** TUESDAY	**29** WEDNESDAY	**30** THURSDAY
1 FRIDAY	2 SATURDAY	3 SUNDAY	4 MONDAY
5 TUESDAY	6 WEDNESDAY	7 THURSDAY	8 FRIDAY

ALL ABOUT SEPTEMBER

I only have the fondest memories of September. Warm evenings. The smell of new copies. Wrapping books in old scraps of wallpaper. Daddy always said I was the only child in Ballygobbard who queued up to go back to school and I've no problem admitting it.

These days September is still my favourite month. All the good telly is back and honestly there are only so many long summer days I can take before I start eyeing up new ankle boots and making soup and thinking about lighting the fire. Of course, lighting the fire in September would be sacrilege, but it doesn't stop my mind wandering and reminiscing about the smell of turf. I'm only human. Don't forget to set your alarm clock twenty minutes earlier to beat the back-to-school traffic.

ALL ABOUT SEPTEMBER

GOALS FOR SEPTEMBER

NEW THINGS TO READ/WATCH/MAKE/EAT

MUST GET DONE

SELF-CARE IDEAS

SEPTEMBER 1–6

30 MONDAY **AUGUST**

31 TUESDAY

1 WEDNESDAY **SEPTEMBER**

2 THURSDAY

3 FRIDAY

SEPTEMBER

4 SATURDAY

5 SUNDAY

IMPORTANT BITS

M	T	W	T	F	S	S
		1	2	3	4	5
6	7	8	9	10	11	12
13	14	15	16	17	18	19
20	21	22	23	24	25	26
27	28	29	30			

SEPTEMBER 6–12

6 MONDAY

7 TUESDAY

8 WEDNESDAY

9 THURSDAY

10 FRIDAY

SEPTEMBER

11 SATURDAY

12 SUNDAY

IMPORTANT BITS

M	T	W	T	F	S	S
		1	2	3	4	5
6	7	8	9	10	11	12
13	14	15	16	17	18	19
20	21	22	23	24	25	26
27	28	29	30			

SEPTEMBER 13–19

13 MONDAY

14 TUESDAY

15 WEDNESDAY NATIONAL PLOUGHING CHAMPIONSHIPS

I never leave the Ploughing without at least four free branded ponchos and the autographs of two RTÉ personalities, minimum.

16 THURSDAY

17 FRIDAY

SEPTEMBER

18 SATURDAY

19 SUNDAY

IMPORTANT BITS

M	T	W	T	F	S	S
		1	2	3	4	5
6	7	8	9	10	11	12
13	14	15	16	17	18	19
20	21	22	23	24	25	26
27	28	29	30			

SEPTEMBER 20–26

20 MONDAY

21 TUESDAY

22 WEDNESDAY

23 THURSDAY

24 FRIDAY INTERNATIONAL WET DARCY DAY

Today marks 26 years since the BBC first broadcast that glorious version of Pride and Prejudice *starring Colin Firth as Mr Darcy. Time for a rewatch?*

SEPTEMBER

25 SATURDAY

26 SUNDAY

IMPORTANT BITS

M	T	W	T	F	S	S
		1	2	3	4	5
6	7	8	9	10	11	12
13	14	15	16	17	18	19
20	21	22	23	24	25	26
27	28	29	30			

SEPTEMBER 27–30

27 MONDAY

28 TUESDAY

29 WEDNESDAY

30 THURSDAY

1 FRIDAY OCTOBER

SEPTEMBER

2 SATURDAY

3 SUNDAY

IMPORTANT BITS

M	T	W	T	F	S	S
		1	2	3	4	5
6	7	8	9	10	11	12
13	14	15	16	17	18	19
20	21	22	23	24	25	26
27	28	29	30			

SEPTEMBER REFLECTIONS

SEPTEMBER REFLECTIONS

If October was a colour
it would be a swirl of gold and
red and orange and fire. Sort
of like Majella's hair when she
goes at it with a bottle of semi-
permanent 'spiced cognac' dye.
A fiesta for the eyes.

October

OCTOBER AT A GLANCE

27 MONDAY	28 TUESDAY	29 WEDNESDAY	30 THURSDAY
1 FRIDAY	**2** SATURDAY	**3** SUNDAY	**4** MONDAY
5 TUESDAY	**6** WEDNESDAY	**7** THURSDAY	**8** FRIDAY
9 SATURDAY	**10** SUNDAY	**11** MONDAY	**12** TUESDAY
13 WEDNESDAY	**14** THURSDAY	**15** FRIDAY	**16** SATURDAY

OCTOBER AT A GLANCE

17 SUNDAY	18 MONDAY	19 TUESDAY	20 WEDNESDAY
21 THURSDAY	22 FRIDAY	23 SATURDAY	24 SUNDAY
25 MONDAY	26 TUESDAY	27 WEDNESDAY	28 THURSDAY
29 FRIDAY	30 SATURDAY	31 SUNDAY	1 MONDAY
2 TUESDAY	3 WEDNESDAY	4 THURSDAY	5 FRIDAY

ALL ABOUT OCTOBER

It's my absolute favourite time of the year: black tights season. I've decided I'm going to go buck wild in 2021 and invest in some M&S hosiery. Sadhbh swears by the longevity of the eighty denier tights and if I'm going to spend €13 on them I want them to see me through to the new year. I love October and the first whiff of a cold snap. I absolutely live for a scarf and hat combo from Penneys and an egg in a cup to warm me up before a crisp, leafy walk.

Halloween has always been a favourite in our house and I'm a purist when it comes to costumes. A black sack and a plastic mask with dangerously sharp nose holes were always good enough for me so I love to see kids putting in a bit of effort, elbow grease and Pritt Stick. I have a bit of PTSD from nearly choking during a fiercely competitive round of Bobbing for Apples with my brother Paul when I was thirteen, but I have been known to be a whizz at Apple on a String. I have my granny's jaw.

ALL ABOUT OCTOBER

GOALS FOR OCTOBER

NEW THINGS TO READ/WATCH/MAKE/EAT

MUST GET DONE

SELF-CARE IDEAS

OCTOBER 1–3

27 MONDAY **SEPTEMBER**

28 TUESDAY

29 WEDNESDAY

30 THURSDAY

1 FRIDAY **OCTOBER**

OCTOBER

2 SATURDAY

3 SUNDAY

IMPORTANT BITS

M	T	W	T	F	S	S
				1	2	3
4	5	6	7	8	9	10
11	12	13	14	15	16	17
18	19	20	21	22	23	24
25	26	27	28	29	30	31

OCTOBER 4–10

4 MONDAY

5 TUESDAY

6 WEDNESDAY

7 THURSDAY

8 FRIDAY

OCTOBER

9 SATURDAY

10 SUNDAY

IMPORTANT BITS

M	T	W	T	F	S	S
				1	2	3
4	5	6	7	8	9	10
11	12	13	14	15	16	17
18	19	20	21	22	23	24
25	26	27	28	29	30	31

OCTOBER 11–17

11 MONDAY

12 TUESDAY

13 WEDNESDAY

14 THURSDAY

15 FRIDAY

OCTOBER

16 SATURDAY

17 SUNDAY

IMPORTANT BITS

M	T	W	T	F	S	S
				1	2	3
4	5	6	7	8	9	10
11	12	13	14	15	16	17
18	19	20	21	22	23	24
25	26	27	28	29	30	31

OCTOBER 18–24

18 MONDAY

19 TUESDAY

20 WEDNESDAY

21 THURSDAY

22 FRIDAY

OCTOBER

23 SATURDAY

24 SUNDAY

IMPORTANT BITS

M	T	W	T	F	S	S
				1	2	3
4	5	6	7	8	9	10
11	12	13	14	15	16	17
18	19	20	21	22	23	24
25	26	27	28	29	30	31

OCTOBER 25–31

25 MONDAY OCTOBER BANK HOLIDAY

The last bank holiday of the year and one of the best if you ask me. Watch You've Got Mail *under a blanket and make popcorn from scratch.*

26 TUESDAY

27 WEDNESDAY

28 THURSDAY

29 FRIDAY REMINDER!

The clocks go back on Saturday night. Don't forget to update the oven, car and microwave. Majella only has hers right for six months of the year and it gives me night terrors.

OCTOBER

30 SATURDAY

31 SUNDAY HALLOWEEN

IMPORTANT BITS

M	T	W	T	F	S	S
				1	2	3
4	5	6	7	8	9	10
11	12	13	14	15	16	17
18	19	20	21	22	23	24
25	26	27	28	29	30	31

OCTOBER REFLECTIONS

OCTOBER REFLECTIONS

In November we remember the loved ones who are no longer with us. We also remember to have de-icer in the glove compartment and that a polo neck never goes out of style.

November

NOVEMBER AT A GLANCE

1 MONDAY	**2** TUESDAY	**3** WEDNESDAY	**4** THURSDAY
5 FRIDAY	**6** SATURDAY	**7** SUNDAY	**8** MONDAY
9 TUESDAY	**10** WEDNESDAY	**11** THURSDAY	**12** FRIDAY
13 SATURDAY	**14** SUNDAY	**15** MONDAY	**16** TUESDAY
17 WEDNESDAY	**18** THURSDAY	**19** FRIDAY	**20** SATURDAY

NOVEMBER AT A GLANCE

21 SUNDAY	**22** MONDAY	**23** TUESDAY	**24** WEDNESDAY
25 THURSDAY	**26** FRIDAY	**27** SATURDAY	**28** SUNDAY
29 MONDAY	**30** TUESDAY	1 WEDNESDAY	2 THURSDAY
3 FRIDAY	4 SATURDAY	5 SUNDAY	6 MONDAY
7 TUESDAY	8 WEDNESDAY	9 THURSDAY	10 FRIDAY

ALL ABOUT NOVEMBER

Coming up to the end of the year, I often find myself getting a bit maudlin. But you're allowed cry about dead people in November. You nearly have to. And remembering is nice and sometimes a cry is almost as good as a holiday. (I'm talking about a good ugly cry with keening and snots, not a single elegant tear like Julia Roberts at the opera in *Pretty Woman*.)

I'm at my most vigilant when the evenings close in. Looking out for black ice, keeping the bird feeder topped up, taking down the number plates of strange cars in case CrimeCall needs me. Idle hands are the devil's tools, as Granny Reilly always said.

ALL ABOUT NOVEMBER

GOALS FOR NOVEMBER

NEW THINGS TO READ/WATCH/MAKE/EAT

MUST GET DONE

SELF-CARE IDEAS

NOVEMBER 1–7

1 MONDAY

2 TUESDAY ALL SOULS' DAY

Stock up on some top-shelf tissues (you're worth the balsam, I promise) and just cry it out. You'll feel all the better for it.

3 WEDNESDAY

4 THURSDAY

5 FRIDAY

NOVEMBER

6 SATURDAY

7 SUNDAY

IMPORTANT BITS

M	T	W	T	F	S	S
1	2	3	4	5	6	7
8	9	10	11	12	13	14
15	16	17	18	19	20	21
22	23	24	25	26	27	28
29	30					

NOVEMBER 8–14

8 MONDAY

9 TUESDAY

10 WEDNESDAY

11 THURSDAY

12 FRIDAY

NOVEMBER

13 SATURDAY

14 SUNDAY

IMPORTANT BITS

M	T	W	T	F	S	S
1	2	3	4	5	6	7
8	9	10	11	12	13	14
15	16	17	18	19	20	21
22	23	24	25	26	27	28
29	30					

NOVEMBER 15–21

15 MONDAY

16 TUESDAY

17 WEDNESDAY

18 THURSDAY

19 FRIDAY

NOVEMBER

20 SATURDAY

21 SUNDAY

IMPORTANT BITS

M	T	W	T	F	S	S
1	2	3	4	5	6	7
8	9	10	11	12	13	14
15	16	17	18	19	20	21
22	23	24	25	26	27	28
29	30					

NOVEMBER 22–28

22 MONDAY

23 TUESDAY

24 WEDNESDAY

25 THURSDAY

26 FRIDAY BLACK FRIDAY

I used to be a demon for the January Sales but it's all about Black Friday now. The deals are off the charts!

NOVEMBER

27 SATURDAY

28 SUNDAY

IMPORTANT BITS

M	T	W	T	F	S	S
1	2	3	4	5	6	7
8	9	10	11	12	13	14
15	16	17	18	19	20	21
22	23	24	25	26	27	28
29	30					

NOVEMBER 29–30

29 MONDAY

30 TUESDAY

1 WEDNESDAY **DECEMBER**

2 THURSDAY

3 FRIDAY

NOVEMBER

4 SATURDAY

5 SUNDAY

IMPORTANT BITS

M	T	W	T	F	S	S
1	2	3	4	5	6	7
8	9	10	11	12	13	14
15	16	17	18	19	20	21
22	23	24	25	26	27	28
29	30					

NOVEMBER REFLECTIONS

NOVEMBER REFLECTIONS

It's beginning to look a lot like ... whatever you want it to be. Decide that this December and this Christmas are going to go your way and you're going to eat as many mini quiches as your heart demands.

December

DECEMBER AT A GLANCE

29 MONDAY	30 TUESDAY	**1** WEDNESDAY	**2** THURSDAY
3 FRIDAY	**4** SATURDAY	**5** SUNDAY	**6** MONDAY
7 TUESDAY	**8** WEDNESDAY	**9** THURSDAY	**10** FRIDAY
11 SATURDAY	**12** SUNDAY	**13** MONDAY	**14** TUESDAY
15 WEDNESDAY	**16** THURSDAY	**17** FRIDAY	**18** SATURDAY

DECEMBER AT A GLANCE

19 SUNDAY	**20** MONDAY	**21** TUESDAY	**22** WEDNESDAY
23 THURSDAY	**24** FRIDAY	**25** SATURDAY	**26** SUNDAY
27 MONDAY	**28** TUESDAY	**29** WEDNESDAY	**30** THURSDAY
31 FRIDAY	1 SATURDAY	2 SUNDAY	3 MONDAY
4 TUESDAY	5 WEDNESDAY	6 THURSDAY	7 FRIDAY

ALL ABOUT DECEMBER

Another year, another failure to secure a place at Newgrange for the Winter Solstice. Niamh from Across the Road has had her ticket for six months and is 'returning for the eighth time' according to her mother. God forgive me but I hope she falls over a cairn or an ogham stone. I was somehow involved in six different Kris Kindle exchanges last year and my heart was broken printing out pictures and buying frames but it's just such a lovely personal gift. I'm taking part in three max this year, and I might pivot to fancy candles. Well, fancy candles in the €15–20 price bracket. I'm not one for going over a Kris Kindle limit. I always loved Christmas and even though we're missing some faces around the table, there's nothing a row over Trivial Pursuit and Mammy going on her ear after two brandies won't fix.

ALL ABOUT DECEMBER

GOALS FOR DECEMBER

NEW THINGS TO READ/WATCH/MAKE/EAT

MUST GET DONE

SELF-CARE IDEAS

DECEMBER 1-5

29 MONDAY **NOVEMBER**

30 TUESDAY

1 WEDNESDAY **DECEMBER**

2 THURSDAY

3 FRIDAY

DECEMBER

4 SATURDAY

5 SUNDAY

IMPORTANT BITS

M	T	W	T	F	S	S
		1	2	3	4	5
6	7	8	9	10	11	12
13	14	15	16	17	18	19
20	21	22	23	24	25	26
27	28	29	30	31		

DECEMBER 6–12

6 MONDAY

7 TUESDAY

8 WEDNESDAY CULCHIE SHOPPING DAY

Online stores and regional shopping meccas have mostly done away with this special tradition, but I always have a ceremonial scone at 11am and imagine I'm in Kylemore Cafe with seven shops already under my belt.

9 THURSDAY

10 FRIDAY

DECEMBER

11 SATURDAY

12 SUNDAY

IMPORTANT BITS

M	T	W	T	F	S	S
		1	2	3	4	5
6	7	8	9	10	11	12
13	14	15	16	17	18	19
20	21	22	23	24	25	26
27	28	29	30	31		

DECEMBER 13–19

13 MONDAY

14 TUESDAY

15 WEDNESDAY

16 THURSDAY

17 FRIDAY

DECEMBER

18 SATURDAY

19 SUNDAY

IMPORTANT BITS

M	T	W	T	F	S	S
		1	2	3	4	5
6	7	8	9	10	11	12
13	14	15	16	17	18	19
20	21	22	23	24	25	26
27	28	29	30	31		

DECEMBER 20–26

20 MONDAY

21 TUESDAY

22 WEDNESDAY

23 THURSDAY

24 FRIDAY CHRISTMAS EVE

DECEMBER

25 SATURDAY CHRISTMAS DAY

26 SUNDAY ST STEPHEN'S DAY
Time to try out the new curling tongs (I won't reduce myself to calling it a wand) and avoid people you shifted in fourth year at the bar. God bless us, every one.

IMPORTANT BITS

M	T	W	T	F	S	S
		1	2	3	4	5
6	7	8	9	10	11	12
13	14	15	16	17	18	19
20	21	22	23	24	25	26
27	28	29	30	31		

DECEMBER 27–31

27 MONDAY

28 TUESDAY

29 WEDNESDAY

30 THURSDAY

31 FRIDAY NEW YEAR'S EVE

I like to light one of my good candles and say a little goodbye to another year gone by. Only for a few minutes, mind. Don't want to be wasting it.

DECEMBER

1 SATURDAY **JANUARY**

2 SUNDAY

IMPORTANT BITS

M	T	W	T	F	S	S
			1	2	3	4	5
6	7	8	9	10	11	12
13	14	15	16	17	18	19
20	21	22	23	24	25	26
27	28	29	30	31		

DECEMBER REFLECTIONS

DECEMBER REFLECTIONS

REFLECTIONS ON MY YEAR

My biggest achievements, challenges and happiest memories

_____
_____
_____
_____
_____
_____
_____
_____
_____
_____
_____
_____
_____
_____
_____
_____
_____
_____
_____
_____
_____
_____
_____

FAVOURITE BOOKS AND MOVIES OF THE YEAR

PRIORITIES FOR 2022

NOTES

NOTES

NOTES

NOTES

NOTES